LITERATURE FROM CRESCENT MOON PUBLISHING

Sexing Hardy: Thomas Hardy and Feminism
by Margaret Elvy

Thomas Hardy's Jude the Obscure: A Critical Study
by Margaret Elvy

Thomas Hardy's Tess of the d'Urbervilles: A Critical Study
by Margaret Elvy

Stepping Forward: Essays, Lectures and Interviews
by Wolfgang Iser

Andrea Dworkin
by Jeremy Mark Robinson

German Romantic Poetry: Goethe, Novalis, Heine, Hölderlin
by Carol Appleby

Rilke: Space, Essence and Angels in the Poetry of Rainer Maria Rilke
by B.D. Barnacle

Rimbaud: Arthur Rimbaud and the Magic of Poetry
by Jeremy Mark Robinson

D.H. Lawrence: Infinite Sensual Violence
by M.K. Pace

D.H. Lawrence: Symbolic Landscapes
by Jane Foster

Samuel Beckett Goes Into the Silence
by Jeremy Mark Robinson

*In the Dim Void: Samuel Beckett's Late Trilogy:
Company, Ill Seen, Ill Said and Worstward Ho*
by Gregory Johns

Andre Gide: Fiction and Fervour in the Novels
by Jeremy Mark Robinson

Amorous Life: John Cowper Powys and the Manifestation of Affectivity
by H.W. Fawkner

Postmodern Powys: New Essays on John Cowper Powys
by Joe Boulter

Rethinking Powys: Critical Essays on John Cowper Powys
edited by Jeremy Mark Robinson

Thomas Hardy and John Cowper Powys: Wessex Revisited
by Jeremy Mark Robinson

Julia Kristeva: Art, Love, Melancholy, Philosophy, Semiotics
by Kelly Ives

Luce Irigaray: Lips, Kissing, and the Politics of Sexual Difference
by Kelly Ives

Helene Cixous I Love You: The Jouissance of Writing
by Kelly Ives

Emily Dickinson: *Selected Poems*
selected and introduced by Miriam Chalk

Petrarch, Dante and the Troubadours: The Religion of Love and Poetry
by Cassidy Hughes

Dante: *Selections From the Vita Nuova*
translated by Thomas Okey

Friedrich Hölderlin: *Selected Poems*
translated by Michael Hamburger

Rainer Maria Rilke: *Selected Poems*
translated by Michael Hamburger

Walking In Cornwall
by Ursula Le Guin

A Great Ring of Pure and Endless Light
Selected Poems

A Great Ring of Pure and Endless Light

Selected Poems

Henry Vaughan

Edited by A.H. Ninham

CRESCENT MOON

CRESCENT MOON PUBLISHING
P.O. Box 1312, Maidstone
Kent, ME14 5XU
United Kingdom

First published 1994. Second edition 2008. Third edition 2025.
Introduction © A.H. Ninham, 1994, 2008, 2025.

Set in Book Antiqua 12 on 15pt.
Designed by Radiance Graphics.

The right of A.H. Ninham to be identified as the editor of *A Great Ring of Pure and Endless Light: Selected Poems* has been asserted generally in accordance with sections 77 and 78 of the Copyright, Designs and Patents Act 1988.

All rights reserved. No part of this book may be reprinted or reproduced, stored in a retrieval system, or transmitted, in any form or by any means, electronic, mechanical, photocopying, recording or otherwise, without permission from the publisher.

British Library Cataloguing in Publication data

Vaughan, Henry
A Great Ring of Pure and Endless Light: Selected Poems.
- (British Poets Series)
I. Title II. Ninham, A.H. III. Series
821.4

ISBN-13 9781861711403
ISBN-13 9798265753687
ISBN-13 9781861719348
ISBN-13 9781861719355

Contents

The World	11
"They are all gone into the world of light!"	14
The Night	16
The Morning-Watch	18
The Retreat	20
To the River Isca	22
The Shower	25
A Fluvium Iscam / To the River Usk	26
Upon the Priory Grove	28
An Epitaph Upon the Lady Elizabeth	30
To My Worthy Friend, Master T. Leaves	32
To My Worthy Friend, Mr Henry Vaughan the Silurist	34
To the Most Excellently Accomplished, Mrs K. Philips	37
To Sir William Davenant	39
To Amoret Gone From Him	41
To Amoret, The Sigh	42
To Amoret, Walking in a Starry Evening	43

To Amoret, of the Difference 'Twixt Him	45
To Amoret Weeping	47
Les Amours	49
To His Friend, Being In Love	51
An Elegy	52
The Charnel-House	53
Song	56
A Rhapsody	57
Fida: Or the Country Beauty, to Lysimachus	60
Fida Forsaken	63
The Character, to Etesia	65
To Etesia Looking From her Casement at the Full Moon	67
To Etesia (For Timander)	68
To Etesia Parted From Him	70
Etesia Absent	71
To Etesia Going Beyond the Sea	72
To His Books	73
Distraction	74
The Eagle	76
Discipline	78
Midnight	79
Peace	81
Mount of Olives (II)	82

Looking Back	83
Retirement	84
The Revival	85
Regeneration	86
The Request	90
The Recovery	92
The Day-Spring	94
The World (II)	96
Introduction	104
Bibliography	110

The World

1

I saw Eternity the other night
Like a great *Ring* of pure and endless light,
    All calm, as it was bright,
And round beneath it, Time in hours, days, years
    Driven by the spheres
Like a vast shadow moved, in which the world
    And all her train were hurled;
The doting lover in his quaintest straing
    Did there complain,
Near him, his lute, his fancy, and his flights,
    Wit's sour delights,
With gloves, and knots the silly snares of pleasure
    Yet his dear treasure
All scattered lay, while he his eyes did pour
    Upon a flower.

2

The darksome states-man hung with weights and woe
Like a thick midnight-fog moved there so slow
    He did nor stay, nor go;
Condemning thoughts (like sad eclipses) scowl
    Upon his soul,
And clouds of crying witnesses without

      Pursued him with one shout.
Yet digged the mole, and lest his ways be found
      Worked under ground,
Where he did clutch his prey, but one did see
      That policy,
Churches and altars fed him, perjuries
      Were gnats and flies,
It rained about him blood and tears, but he
      Drank them as free.

3

The fearful miser on a heap of rust
Sat pining all his life there, did scarce trust
      His own hands with the dust,
Yet would not place one piece above, but lives
      In fear of thieves.
Thousands there were as frantic as himself
      And hugged each one his pelf,
The down-right epicure placed heaven in sense
      And scorned pretence
While others slipped into a wide excess
      Said little less;
The weaker sort slight, trivial wares enslave
      Who think them brave,
And poor, despised truth sat counting by
      Their victory.

4

Yet some, who all this while did weep and sing,
And sing, and weep, soared up into the *Ring*,
    But most would use no wing.
O fools (said I,) thus to prefer dark night
    Before true light,
To live in grots, and caves, and hate the day
    Because it shows the way,
The way which from this dead and dark abode
    Leads up to God,
A way where you might tread the sun, and he
    More bright than he.
But as I did their madness so discuss
    One whispered thus,
This ring the bride-groom did for none provide
    But for his bride.

'They are all gone into the world of light!'

They are all gone into the world of light!
    And I alone sit ling'ring here;
Their very memory is fair and bright,
    And my sad thoughts doth clear.

It glows and glitters in my cloudy breast
    Like stars upon some gloomy grove,
Or those faint beams in which this hill is dressed,
    After the sun's remove.

I see them walking in an air of glory,
    Whose light doth trample on my days:
My days, which are at best but dull and hoary,
    Mere glimmering and decays.

O holy hope! and high humility,
    High as the heavens above!
These are your walks, and you have showed them me
    To kindle my cold love,

Dear, beauteous death! the jewel of the just,

Shining nowhere, but in the dark;
What mysteries do lie beyond thy dust;
    Could man outlook that mark!

He that hath found some fledged bird's nest, may know
    At first sight, if the bird be flown;
But what fair well, or grove he sings in now,
    That is to him unknown.

And yet, as Angels in some brighter dreams
    Call to the soul, when man doth sleep:
So some strange thoughts transcend our wonted themes,
    And into glory peep.

If a star were confined into a tomb
    Her captive flames must needs burn there;
But when the hand that locked her up, gives room
    She'll shine through all the sphere.

Of Father of eternal life, and all
    Created glories under thee!
Resume thy spirit from this world of thrall
    Into true liberty.

Either disperse these mists, which blot and fill
    My perspective (still) as they pass,
Or else remove me hence unto that hill,
    Where I shall need no glass.

The Night

    Through that pure *Virgin-shrine*,
That sacred veil drawn o'er thy glorious noon
That men might look and live as glow-worms shine,
      And face the moon:
   Wise *Nicodemus* saw such light
   As made him know his God by night.

    Most blest believer he!
Who in that land of darkness and blind eyes
Thy long expected healing wings could see,
      When thou didst rise,
   And what can nevermore be done,
   Did at mid-night speak with the Sun!

    O who will tell me, where
He found thee at that dead and silent hour!
What hallowed solitary ground did bear
      So rare a flower,
   Within whose sacred leaves did lie
   The fullness of the Deity.

    No mercy-seat of gold,
No dead and dusty *Cherub*, nor carved stone,
But his own living works did my Lord hold
      And lodge alone;
   Where *trees* and *herbs* did watch and peep
   And wounds, while the *Jews* did sleep.

    Dear night! this world's defeat;

The stop to busy fools; care's check and curb;
The day of Spirits; my soul's calm retreat
      Which none disturb!
  Christ's progress, and his prayer time;
  The hours to which high Heaven doth chime.

    God's silent, searching flight:
When my Lord's head is filled with dew, and all
His locks are wet with the clear drops of night;
      His still,s oft call;
  His knocking time; the soul's dumb watch,
  When Spirits their fair kindred catch.

    Were all my loud, evil days
Calm and unhaunted as is thy dark Tent,
Whose peace but by some *Angel's* wing or voice
      Is seldom rent;
  Then I in Heaven all the long year
  Would keep, and never wander here.

    But living where the sun
Doth all things wake, and where all mix and tire
Themselves and others,I consent and run
      To every mire,
  And by this world's ill-guiding light,
  Err more than I can do by night.

    There is in God (some say)
A deep, but dazzling darkness; as men here
Say it is late and dusky, because they
      See not all clear;
  O for that night! where I in him
  Might live invisible and dim.

The Morning-Watch

O joys! infinite sweetness! with what flowers,
And shoots of glory, my soul breaks, and buds!
      All the long hours
      Of night, and rest
      Through the still shrouds
      Of sleep, and clouds,
    This dew fell on my breast;
      Of how it *blows*,
And *spirits* all my earth! hark! In what rings,
And *hymning circulations* the quick world
      Awakes, and sings;
      The rising winds,
      And falling springs,
      Birds, beasts, all things
    A doe him in their kinds.
    Thus all is hurled
In sacred *hymns*, and *order*, the great *chime*
And *symphony* of nature. Prayer is
      The world in tune,
      A spirit-voice,
      And vocal joys
    Whose *echo is* heaven's bliss.
  O let me climb
When I lie down! The pious soul by night

Is like a clouded star, whose beams though said
        To shed their light
        Under some cloud
           Yet are above,
           And shine, and move
        Beyond that misty shroud.
          So in my bed
That curtained grave, though sleep, like ashes, hide
My lamp, and life, both shall in thee abide.

The Retreat

Happy those early days! when I
Shined in my Angel-infancy.
Before I understood this place
Appointed for my second race,
Or taught my soul to fancy aught
But a white, celestial thought,
When yet I had not walked above
A mile, or two, from my first love,
And looking back (at that short space,)
Could see a glimpse of his bright-face;
When on some *gilded cloud,* or *flower*
My gazing souls would dwell an hour,
And in those weaker glories spy
Some shadows of eternity;
Before I taught my tongue to wound
My conscience with a sinful sound,
Or had the black art to dispense
A several sin to every sense,
But felt through all this fleshly dress
Bright *shoots* of everlastingness.
   O how I long to travel back
And tread against hat ancient track!
That I might once more reach that plain,
Where first I left my glorious train,
From whence the enlightened spirits sees
That shady city of palm trees;
But (ah!) my soul with too much stay

Is drunk, and staggers in the way.
Some men a forward motion love,
But I by backward steps would move,
And when this dust falls to the urn
In that state I came return.

To the River Isca

When *Daphne's* lover here first wore the *bays*,
Eurotas' secret streams heard all his *lays*,
And holy *Orpheus*, Nature's *busy* child,
By headlong *Hebrus* his deep *hymns* compil'd;
Soft *Petrarch* – thaw'd by *Laura's* flames – did weep
On *Tiber's* banks, when she – *proud fair!* – could sleep;
Mosella boasts *Ausonius*, and the *Thames*
Doth murmur *Sidney's Stell*a to her *streams*;
While *Severn*, swoln with *joy* and *sorrow*, wears
Castara's smiles mix'd with fair *Sabrin's* tears.
Thus *poets* – like the *nymphs*, their *pleasing themes* –
Haunted the *bubbling springs* and *gliding streams*;
And *happy banks*! whence such *fair flow'rs* have
                    sprung,
But happier those where they have *sat* and *sung*!
Poets – like *angels* – where they once appear
Hallow the *place*, and each succeeding year
Adds *rev'rence* to't, such as at length doth give
This aged faith, *that there their genii live.*
Hence th' *ancients* say, that from this *sickly air*
They pass to *regions* more *refin'd* and *fair*,
To *meadows* strew'd with *lilies* and the *rose*,
And *shades* whose *youthful green* no *old age* knows;
Where all in *white* they walk, discourse, and sing
Like bees' *soft murmurs*, or a *chiding spring*.
   But *Isca*, whensoe'er those *shades* I see,
And thy *lov'd arbours* must no more *know* me,

When I am laid to *rest* hard by thy *streams*,
And my *sun sets*, where first it *sprang* in beams,
I'll leave behind me such a *large, kind light*,
As shall *redeem* thee from *oblivious* night,
And in these *vows* which – living yet – I pay,
Shed such a *previous* and *enduring ray*,
As shall from age to age thy *fair name* lead,
'Till *rivers* leave to *run*, and *men* to *read*.
First, may all *bards* born after me
 – When I am *ashes* – sing of thee!
May thy *green banks* or *streams*, – or none –
Be both their *hill* and *Helicon*!
May *vocal groves* grow there, and all
The *shades* in them *prophetical*,
Where laid men shall more *fair truths* see
Than *fictions* were of *Thessaly*!
May thy gentle *swains* – like *flow'rs* –
Sweetly spend their *youthful hours*,
And thy *beauteous nymphs* – like *doves* –
Be *kind* and *faithful* to their *loves*!
Garlands, and *songs*, and *roundelays*,
Mild, dewy *nights*, and sunshine *days*,
The *turtle's voice, joy* without *fear*,
Dwell on thy *bosom* all the year!
May the *evet* and the *toad*
Within thy banks have no abode,
Nor the *wily, winding snake*
Her *voyage* through thy *waters* make!
In all thy *journey* to the *main*
No *nitrous clay*, nor *brimstone-vein*
Mix with thy *streams*, but may they pass
Fresh on the *air*, and clear as *glass*,
And where the *wand'ring crystal* treads

Roses shall *kiss*, and *couple* heads!
The *factor-wind* from far shall bring
The *odours* of the *scatter'd* Spring,
And *loaden* with the rich *arrear*,
Spend it in *spicy whispers* there.
No *sullen heats*, nor *flames* that are
Offensive, and *canicular*,
Shine on thy *sands*, nor *pry* to see
Thy *scaly, shading family,*
But *noons* as mild as *Hesper's* rays,
Or the first *blushes* of fair days!
What *gifts* more *Heav'n* or *Earth* can add,
With all those *blessings* be thou *clad*!
    Honour, Beauty,
    Faith and *Duty,*
    Delight and *Truth,*
    With *Love* and *Youth,*
Crown all about thee! and whatever *Fate*
Impose elsewhere, whether the graver state
Or some toy else, may those *loud, anxious* cares
For *dead* and *dying things* – the common wares
And *shows* of Time – ne'er break thy *peace*, nor make
Thy *repos'd* arms to a new war *awake*!
    But *freedom, safety, joy* and *bliss,*
    United in one loving *kiss,*
    Surround thee quite, and *style* thy borders
  The land redeem'd from all disorders!

The Shower

Waters above! eternal springs!
The dew that silvers the Dove's wings!
O welcome, welcome to the sad!
Give dry dust drink; drink that makes glad!
Many fair ev'nings, many flow'rs
Sweeten'd with rich and gentle showers,
Have I enjoy'd, and down have run
Many a fine and shining sun;
But never, till this happy hour,
Was blest with such an evening-shower!

A Fluvium Iscam

Isca parens florum, placido qui spumens ore
*   Lambis lapillos aureos,*
Qui maestos hyacinthos, et picti tophi
*   Mulces susurris humidis,*
Dumque novas *pergunt* menses *consumere* lunas
*   Coelumque* mortales *terit,*
Accumulas cum sole *dies, aevumque per omne*
*   Fidelis* induras *latex,*
O quis inaccessos et quali murmure lucos
*   Mutumque* solaris *nemus!*
Per te discerpti credo Thracis *ire querelas*
Plectrumque divini sensis.

To the River Usk

Usk, father of flowers, foaming from your quiet spring, you lap the golden pebbles, and with your moist murmurings soothe the sorrowful hyacinths and the flora on the colourful rock; and while the months run on to engulf new moons, and heaven wears down mortal men, you number your days with the sun, and last out every age, an unfailing stream. What comfort you bring to the remote woods and the silent grove, and with what a murmurous whisper! I believe that the plaints of the dismembered Thracian move along your waters, and the lyre of the divine old man.

Upon the Priory Grove, His Usual Retirement

Hail, sacred shades! cool, leafy house!
Chaste treasurer of all my vows
And wealth! on whose soft bosom laid
My love's fair steps I first betray'd:
   Henceforth no melancholy flight,
No sad wing, or hoarse bird of night,
Disturb this air, no fatal throat
Of raven, or owl, awake the note
Of our laid echo, no voice dwell
Within these leaves, but Philomel.
The poisonous ivy here no more
His false twists on the oak shall score;
Only the woodbine here may twine,
As th' emblem of her love, and mine;
The amorous sun shall here convey
His best beams, in thy shades to play;
The active air the gentlest show'rs
Shall from his wings rain on thy flowers;
And the moon from her dewy locks
Shall deck thee with her brightest drops.
Whatever can a fancy move,

Or feed the eye, be on this grove!

   And when at last the winds and tears
Of heaven, with the consuming years,
Shall these green curls bring to decay,
And clothe thee in an aged grey
 – If ought a lover can foresee,
Or if we poets prophets be –
From hence transplanted, thou shalt stand
A fresh grove in th' Elysian land;
Where – most bless'd pair! – as here on earth
Thou first didst eye our growth, and birth;
So there again, thou'lt see us move
In our first innocence and love;
And in thy shades, as now, so then,
We'll kiss, and smile, and walk again.

An Epitaph Upon the Lady Elizabeth, Second Daughter to His Late Majesty

Youth, Beauty, Virtue, Innocence
Heaven's royal, and select expense,
With virgin-tears, and sighs divine,
Sit here the *genii* of this shrine,
Where now (thy fair soul winged away,)
They guard the casket where she lay.
    Thou hadst, ere thou the light couldst see,
Sorrows laid up, and stored for thee,
Thou suck'dst in woes, and the *breasts* lent
Their *milk* to thee, but to lament;
Thy portion here was *grief,* thy years
Distilled no other rain, but tears,
Tears without noise, but (understood)
As loud, and shrill as any blood;
Thou seem'st a *rose-bud* born in *snow,*
A flower of purpose sprung to bow
To headless tempests, and the rage
Of an incensed, stormy age.

Others, ere their afflictions grow,
Are timed, and seasoned for the blow,
But thine, as *rheums* the tenderest part,
Fell on a *young* and *harmless* heart.
And yet as *balm-trees* gently spend
Their tears for those, that do them rend,
So mild and pious thou wert seen,
Though full of *sufferings,* free from *spleen,*
Thou didst nor murmur, nor revile,
But drank'st thy *wormwood* with a *smile,*
As envious eyes blast, and infect
And cause misfortunes by aspect,
So thy sad stars dispensed to thee
No influx, but calamity,
They viewed thee with *eclipsed* rays,
And but the *back-side* of bright days.

• • •

These were the comforts she had here,
As by an unseen hand 'tis clear,
Which now she reads, and smiling wears
A crown with him, who wipes off tears.

To My Worthy Friend, Master T. Lewes

Sees not my friend, what a deep snow
Candies our country's woody brow?
The yielding branch his load scarce bears
Oppressed with snow, and *frozen tears*,
While the *dumb* rivers slowly float,
All bound up in an *icy coat*.
   Let us meet then! and while this world
In wild *eccentrics* now is hurled,
Keep we, like nature, the same *key*,
And walk in our forefathers' way;
Why any more cast we an eye
On what *may come*, not what is *nigh*?
Why vex our selves with *fear*, or *hope*
And cares beyond our *horoscope*?
Who into future times would peer
Looks oft beyond his term set here,
And cannot go into those grounds
But through a *church-yard* which them bounds;
Sorrows and sighs and searches spend
And draw our bottom to an end,
But discreet joys lengthen the lease

Without which life were a disease,
And who this age a mourner goes,
Doth with is tears but feed his foes.

To My Worthy Friend, Mr Henry Vaughan the Silurist

See what thou wert! by what Platonic round
Art thou in thy first youth and glories found?
Or from thy Muse does this retrieve accrue?
Does she which once inspir'd thee, now renew,
Bringing thee back those golden years which Time
Smooth'd to thy lays, and polish'd with thy rhyme?
Nor is't to thee alone she does convey
Such happy change, but bountiful as day,
On whatsoever reader she does shine,
She makes him like thee, and for ever thine.
And first thy manual op'ning gives to see
Eclipse and suff'rings burnish majesty,
Where thou so artfully the draught hast made
That we best read the lustre in the shade,
And find our sov'reign greater in that shroud:
So lightning dazzles from its night and cloud,
So the *First Light Himself* has for His throne
Blackness, and darkness his pavilion.

Who can refuse thee company, or stay,
By thy next charming summons forc'd away,
If that be force which we can so resent,
That only in its joys 'tis violent:
Upward thy *Eagle* bears us ere aware,
Till above storms and all tempestuous air
We radiant worlds with their bright people meet,
Leaving this little *all* beneath our feet.
But now the pleasure is too great to tell,
Nor have we other bus'ness than to dwell,
As on the hallow'd Mount th' Apostles meant
To build and fix their glorious banishment.
Yet we must know and find thy skilful vein
Shall gently bear us to our homes again;
By which descent thy former flight's impli'd
To be thy ecstacy and not thy pride.
And here how well does the wise *Muse* demean
Herself, and fit her song to ev'ry scene!
Riot of courts, the bloody wreaths of war,
Cheats of the mart, and clamours of the bar,
Nay, life itself thou dost so well express,
Its hollow joys, and real emptiness,
That *Dorian* minstrel never did excite,
Or raise for dying so much appetite.

Nor does thy other softer magic move
Us less thy fam'd *Etesia* to love;
Where such a *character* thou giv'st, that shame
Nor envy dare approach the vestal dame:
So at bright prime *ideas* none repine,
They safely in th' *eternal poet* shine.

Gladly th' *Assyrian phœnix* now resumes

From thee this last reprisal of his plumes;
He seems another more miraculous thing,
Brighter of crest, and stronger of his wing,
Proof against Fate in spicy urns to come,
Immortal past all risk of martyrdom.

Nor be concern'd, nor fancy thou art rude
T' adventure from thy Cambrian solitude:
Best from those lofty cliffs thy *Muse* does spring
Upwards, and boldly spreads her cherub wing.
So when the *sage* of *Memphis* would converse
With boding skies, and th' azure universe,
He climbs his starry pyramid, and thence
Freely sucks clean prophetic influence,
And all serene, and rapt and gay he pries
Through the ethereal volume's mysteries,
Loth to come down, or ever to know more
The *Nile's* luxurious, but dull foggy shore.

I. W., A.M. Oxon.

To the Most Excellently Accomplished, Mrs K. Philips

Say, witty fair one, from what sphere
Flow these rich numbers you shed here?
For sure such *incantations* come
From thence, which strike your readers dumb.
A strain, whose measures gently meet
Like *virgin-lovers* or Time's *feet*;
Where language *smiles*, and accents rise
As quick and pleasing as your *eyes*;
The *poem* smooth, and in each line
Soft as *yourself*, yet *masculine*;
Where not coarse trifles blot the page
With matter borrow'd from the age,
But thoughts as innocent and high
As *angels* have, or *saints* that die.
   These raptures when I first did see
New miracles in poetry,
And by a hand their good would miss
His *bays* and *fountains* but to kiss,

My weaker *genius* – cross to fashion –
Slept in a silent admiration:
A rescue, by whose grave disguise
Pretenders oft have pass'd for wise.
And yet as *pilgrims* humbly touch
Those *shrines* to which they bow so much,
And clouds in courtship flock, and run
To be the mask unto the sun,
So I concluded it was true
I might at distance worship you,
A *Persian* votary, and say
It was your light show'd me the way.
So *loadstones* guide the duller *steel*,
And high perfections are the *wheel*
Which moves the less, for gifts divine
Are strung upon a *vital line*,
Which, touch'd by you, excites in all
Affections *epidemical.*
And this made me – a truth most fit –
Add my weak *echo* to your wit;
Which pardon, Lady, for assays
Obscure as these might blast your bays;
As common hands soil *flow'rs*, and make
That dew they wear *weep* the mistake.
But I'll wash off the *stain*, and vow
No *laurel* grows but for your *brow*.

To Sir William Davenant Upon His Gondibert

Well, we are rescued! and by thy rare pen
Poets shall live, when princes die like men.
Th' hast clear'd the prospect to our harmless hill,
Of late years clouded with imputed ill,
And the soft, youthful couples there may move,
As chaste as stars converse and smile above.
Th' hast taught their language and their love to flow
Calm as rose-leaves, and cool as virgin-snow,
Which doubly feasts us, being so refin'd,
They both delight and dignify the mind;
Like to the wat'ry music of some spring,
Whose pleasant flowings at once wash and sing.
   And where before heroic poems were
Made up of spirits, prodigies, and fear,
And show'd – through all the melancholy flight –
Like some dark region overcast with night,
As if the poet had been quite dismay'd,
While only giants and enchantments sway'd;
Thou like the sun, whose eye brooks no disguise,
Hast chas'd them hence, and with discoveries
So rare and learnèd fill'd the place, that we

Those fam'd grandezas find outdone by thee,
And underfoot see all those vizards hurl'd
Which bred the wonder of the former world.
'Twas dull to sit, as our forefathers did,
At crumbs and voiders, and because unbid,
Refrain wise appetite. This made thy fire
Break through the ashes of thy aged sire,
To lend the world such a convincing light
As shows his fancy darker than his sight.
Nor was't alone the bars and length of days
 – Though those gave strength and stature to his bays –
Encounter'd thee, but what's an old complaint
And kills the fancy, a forlorn restraint.
How couldst thou, mur'd in solitary stones,
Dress Birtha's smiles, though well thou mightst her
                              groans?
And, strangely eloquent, thyself divide
'Twixt sad misfortunes and a bloomy bride?
Through all the tenour of thy ample song,
Spun from thy own rich store, and shar'd among
Those fair adventurers, we plainly see
Th' imputed gifts inherent are in thee.
Then live for ever – and by high desert –
In thy own mirror, matchless Gondibert,
And in bright Birtha leave thy love enshrin'd
Fresh as her em'rald, and fair as her mind,
While all confess thee – as they ought to do –
The prince of poets, and of lovers too.

To Amoret Gone From Him

Fancy and I, last evening, walk'd,
And Amoret, of thee we talk'd;
The West just then had stolen the sun,
And his last blushes were begun:
We sate, and mark'd how everything
Did mourn his absence: how the spring
That smil'd and curl'd about his beams,
Whilst he was here, now check'd her streams:
The wanton eddies of her face
Were taught less noise, and smoother grace;
And in a slow, sad channel went,
Whisp'ring the banks their discontent:
The careless ranks of flowers that spread
Their perfum'd bosoms to his head.
And with an open, free embrace,
Did entertain his beamy face,
Like absent friends point to the West,
And on that weak reflection feast.
If creatures then that have no sense,
But the loose tie of influence,
Though fate and time each day remove
Those things that element their love,
At such vast distance can agree,
Why, Amoret, why should not we?

To Amoret, The Sigh

Nimble sigh, on thy warm wings,
   Take this message and depart;
Tell *Amoret*, that smiles and sings,
At what thy airy voyage brings,
   That thou cam'st lately from my heart.

Tell my lovely foe that I
   Have no more such spies to send,
But one or two that I intend,
Some few minutes ere I die,
   To her white bosom to commend.

Then whisper by that holy spring,
   Where for her sake I would have died,
Whilst those water-nymphs did bring
   Flowers to cure what she had tried;
And of my faith and love did sing.

That if my *Amoret*, if she
   In after-times would have it read,
How her beauty murder'd me,
With all my heart I will agree,
   If she'll but love me, being dead.

To Amoret, Walking in a Starry Evening

If *Amoret*, that glorious eye,
    In the first birth of light,
        And death of night,
Had with those elder fires you spy
    Scattered so high
      Received form, and sight;

We might suspect in the vast Ring,
    Amidst these golden glories,
      And fiery stories;
Whether the Sun had been the King,
    And guide of Day,
      Or your brighter eye should sway;

But, *Amoret,* such is my fate,
    That if thy face a Star
      Had shined from far,
I am persuaded in that state
    'Twixt thee, and me,
      Of some predestined sympathy.

For sure such two conspiring minds,
　　Which no accident, or sight,
　　　　Did thus unite;
Whom no distance can confine,
　　　　Start, or decline,
One, for another, were designed.

To Amoret, of the Difference 'Twixt Him, and Other Lovers, and What True Love Is

Mark, when the evening's cooler wings
   Fan the afflicted air, how the faint sun,
     Leaving undone,
     What he begun,
Those spurious flames suck'd up from slime and earth
     To their first, low birth,
     Resigns, and brings.

They shoot their tinsel beams and vanities,
   Threading with those false fires their way;
     But as you stay
     And see them stray,
You lose the flaming track, and subtly they
     Languish away,
     And cheat your eyes.

Just so base, sublunary lovers' hearts
    Fed on loose profane desires,
        May for an eye
        Or face comply:
But those remov'd, they will as soon depart,
        And show their art,
        And painted fires.

To Amoret Weeping

Leave, *Amoret*, melt not away so fast
Thy eyes' fair treasure; Fortune's wealthiest cast
Deserves not one such pearl; for these, well spent,
Can purchase stars, and buy a tenement
For us in heaven; though here the pious streams
Avail us not; who from that clue of sunbeams
Could ever steal one thread? or with a kind
Persuasive accent charm the wild loud wind?

   Fate cuts us all in marble, and the Book
Forestalls our glass of minutes; we may look
But seldom meet a change; think you a tear
Can blot the flinty volume? shall our fear
Or grief add to their triumphs? and must we
Give an advantage to adversity?
Dear, idle prodigal! is it not just
We bear our stars? What though I had not dust
Enough to cabinet a worm? nor stand
Enslav'd unto a little dirt, or sand?
I boast a better purchase, and can show
The glories of a soul that's simply true.

   But grant some richer planet at my birth
Had spied me out, and measur'd so much earth
Or gold unto my share: I should have been
Slave to these lower elements, and seen
My high-born soul flag with their dross, and lie
A pris'ner to base mud, and alchemy.
I should perhaps eat orphans, and suck up

A dozen distress'd widows in one cup;
Nay, further, I should by that lawful stealth,
Damn'd usury, undo the commonwealth;
Or patent it in soap, and coals, and so
Have the smiths curse me, and my laundress too;
Geld wine, or his friend tobacco; and so bring
The incens'd subject rebel to his king;
And after all – as those first sinners fell –
Sink lower than my gold, and lie in hell.
    Thanks then for this deliv'rance! blessed pow'rs,
You that dispense man's fortune and his hours,
How am I to you all engag'd! that thus
By such strange means, almost miraculous,
You should preserve me; you have gone the way
To make me rich by taking all away.
For I – had I been rich – as sure as fate,
Would have been meddling with the king, or State,
Or something to undo me; and 'tis fit,
We know, that who hath wealth should have no wit,
But, above all, thanks to that Providence
That arm'd me with a gallant soul, and sense,
'Gainst all misfortunes, that hath breath'd so much
Of Heav'n into me, that I scorn the touch
Of these low things; and can with courage dare
Whatever fate or malice can prepare:
I envy no man's purse or mines: I know
That, losing them, I've lost their curses too;
And *Amoret* – although our share in these
Is not contemptible, nor doth much please –
Yet, whilst content and love we jointly vie,
    We have a blessing which no gold can buy.

Les Amours

Tyrant farewell: this heart, the prize
And triumph of thy scornful eyes,
I sacrifice to heaven, and give
To quit my sins, that durst believe
A woman's easy faith, and place
True joys in a changing face.
   Yet ere I go; by all those tears,
And sighs I spent 'twixt hopes, and fears;
By thy own glories, and that hour
Which first enslaved me to thy power;
I beg, fair one, by this last breath,
This tribute from thee after death.
If when I'm gone, you chance to see
That cold bed where I lodged be:
Let not your hate in death appear,
But bless my ashes with a tear:
This influx from that quickening eye,
By secret power, which none can spy,
The cold dust shall inform, and make
Those flames (though dead) new life partake.
Whose warmth helped by your tears shall bring,
O'er all the tomb a sudden spring
Of crimson flowers, whose drooping heads
Shall curtain o'er their mournful beds:
And on each leaf by Heaven's command,
These emblems to the life shall stand:
   Two hearts, the first a shaft withstood;

The second, shot, and washed in blood;
And on this heart a dew shall stay,
Which no heat can court away;
But fixed for ever witness bears,
That hearty sorrow feeds on tears.
    Thus Heaven can make it known, and true,
    That you killed me, 'cause I loved you.

To His Friend, Being In Love

Ask, lover, ere thou diest; let one poor breath
Steal from thy lips, to tell her of thy death;
Doating idolater! can silence bring
Thy saint propitious? or will *Cupid* fling
One arrow for thy paleness? leave to try
This silent courtship of a sickly eye.
Witty to tyranny, she too well knows
This but the incense of thy private vows,
That breaks forth at thine eyes, and doth betray
The sacrifice thy wounded heart would pay;
Ask her, fool, ask her; if words cannot move,
The language of thy tears may make her love.

   Flow nimbly from me then; and when you fall
On her breast's warmer snow, O may you all,
By some strange fate fix'd there, distinctly lie,
The much lov'd volume of my tragedy.

   Where, if you win her not, may this be read,
The cold that freez'd you so, did strike me dead.

An Elegy

'Tis true, I am undone: yet, ere I die,
I'll leave these sighs and tears a legacy
To after-lovers: that, rememb'ring me,
Those sickly flames which now benighted be,
Fann'd by their warmer sighs, may love; and prove
In them the metempsychosis of love.
'Twas I – when others scorn'd – vow'd you were fair,
And sware that breath enrich'd the coarser air,
Lent roses to your cheeks, made Flora bring
Her nymphs with all the glories of the spring
To wait upon thy face, and gave my heart
A pledge to *Cupid* for a quicker dart,
To arm those eyes against myself; to me
Thou ow'st that tongue's bewitching harmony.
I courted angels from those upper joys,
And made them leave their spheres to hear thy voice.
I made the Indian curse the hours he spent
To seek his pearls, and wisely to repent
His former folly, and confess a sin,
Charm'd by the brighter lustre of thy skin.
I borrow'd from the winds the gentler wing
Of *Zephyrus*, and soft souls of the spring;
And made – to air those cheeks with fresher grace –
The warm inspirers dwell upon thy face.

Oh! jam satis

The Charnel-House

Bless me! what damps are here! how stiff an air!
Kelder of mists, a second *fiat's* care,
Front'spiece o' th' grave and darkness, a display
Of ruin'd man, and the disease of day,
Lean, bloodless shamble, where I can descry
Fragments of men, rags of anatomy,
Corruption's wardrobe, the transplantive bed
Of mankind, and th' exchequer of the dead!
How thou arrests my sense! how with the sight
My *winter'd* blood grows stiff to all delight!
Torpedo to the eye! whose least glance can
Freeze our wild lusts, and rescue headlong man.
Eloquent silence! able to immure
An *atheist's* thoughts, and blast an *epicure*.
Were I a *Lucian*, Nature in this dress
Would make me wish a Saviour, and confess.
   Where are you, shoreless thoughts, vast tenter'd
                                      hope,
Ambitious dreams, *aims* of an endless scope,
Whose stretch'd excess runs on a string too high,
And on the rack of self-extension die?
Chameleons of state, air-monging band,
Whose breath – like gunpowder – blows up a land,
Come see your dissolution, and weigh
What a loath'd nothing you shall be one day.
As th' elements by circulation pass
From one to th' other, and that which first was

I so again, so 'tis with you; the grave
And Nature but complot; what the one gave
The other takes; think, then, that in this bed
There sleep the relics of as proud a head,
As stern and subtle as your own, that hath
Perform'd, or forc'd as much, whose tempest-wrath
Hath levell'd kings with slaves, and wisely then
Calm these high furies, and descend to men.
Thus *Cyrus* tam'd the *Macedon*; a tomb
Check'd him, who thought the world too straight a
                                      room.

    Have I obey'd the *powers* of face,
A beauty able to undo the race
Of easy man? I look but here, and straight
I am inform'd, the lovely counterfeit
Was but a smoother clay. That famish'd slave
Beggar'd by wealth, who starves that he may save,
Brings hither but his sheet; nay, th' *ostrich-man*
That feeds on *steel* and *bullet*, he that can
Outswear his *lordship*, and reply as tough
To a kind word, as if his tongue were *buff*,
Is *chap*-fall'n here: worms without wit or fear
Defy him now; Death hath disarm'd the *bear*.
Thus could I run o'er all the piteous score
Of erring men, and having done, meet more,
Their shuffled *wills*, abortive, vain *intents*,
Fantastic *humours*, perilous *ascents*,
False, empty *honours*, traitorous *delights*,
And whatsoe'er a blind conceit invites;
But these and more which the weak vermins swell,
Are couch'd in this accumulative cell,
Which I could scatter; but the grudging sun
Calls home his beams, and warns me to be gone;

Day leaves me in a double night, and I
Must bid farewell to my sad library.
Yet with these notes – Henceforth with thought of thee
I'll season all succeeding jollity,
Yet damn not mirth, nor think too much is fit;
Excess hath no *religion*, nor *wit*;
But should wild blood swell to a lawless strain,
One check from thee shall *channel* it again.

Song

Amyntas *go, thou art undone,*
   Thy faithful heart is cross'd by fate;
That love is better not begun,
   Where love is come to love too late.
Had she professèd hidden fires,
   Or show'd one knot that tied her heart,
I could have quench'd my first desires,
   And we had only met to part.
But, tyrant, thus to murder men,
   And shed a lover's harmless blood,
And burn him in those flames again,
   Which he at first might have withstood.
Yet, who that saw fair Chloris *weep*
   Such sacred dew, with such pure grace;
Durst think them feignèd tears, or seek
   For treason in an angel's face.
This is her art, though this be true,
   Men's joys are kill'd with griefs and fears,
Yet she, like flowers oppress'd with dew,
   Doth thrive and flourish in her tears.

A Rhapsody

Occasionally written upon a meeting with some of his friends at the Globe Tavern, in a chamber painted overhead with a cloudy sky and some few dispersed stars, and on the sides with landscapes, hills, shepherds and sheep.

Darkness, and stars i's th' mid-day! They invite
Our active fancies to believe it night:
For taverns need no sun, but for a sign,
Where rich tobacco and quick tapers shine;
And royal, witty sack, the poet's soul,
With brighter suns than he doth gild the bowl;
As though the pot and poet did agree,
Sack should to both illuminator be.
That artificial cloud, with its curl'd brow,
Tells us 'tis late; and that blue space below
Is fir'd with many stars: mark! how they break
In silent glances o'er the hills, and speak
The evening to the plains, where, shot from far,
They meet in dumb salutes, as one great star.
   The room, methinks, grows darker; and the air
Contracts a sadder colour, and less fair.
Or is't the drawer's skill? hath he no arts
To blind us so we can't know pints from quarts?
No, no, 'tis night: look where the jolly clown
Musters his bleating herd and quits the down.

Hark! how his rude pipe frets the quiet air,
Whilst ev'ry hill proclaims *Lycoris* fair.
Rich, happy man! that canst thus watch and sleep,
Free from all cares, but thy wench, pipe and sheep!
    But see, the moon is up; view, where she stands
Sentinel o'er the door, drawn by the hands
Of some base painter, that for gain hath made
Her face the landmark to the tippling trade.
This cup to her, that to *Endymion* give;
'Twas wit at first, and wine that made them live.
Choke may the painter! and his box disclose
No other colours than his fiery nose;
And may we no more of his pencil see
Than two churchwardens, and mortality.
    Should we go now a-wand'ring, we should meet
With catchpoles, whores and carts in ev'ry street:
Now when each narrow lane, each nook and cave,
Sign-posts and shop-doors, pimp for ev'ry knave,
When riotous sinful plush, and tell-tale spurs
Walk Fleet Street and the Strand, when the soft stirs
Of bawdy, ruffled silks, turn night to day;
And the loud whip and coach scolds all the way;
When lust of all sorts, and each itchy blood
From the Tower-wharf to Cymbeline, and Lud,
Hunts for a mate, and the tir'd footman reels
'Twixt chairmen, torches, and the hackney wheels.
    Come, take the other dish; it is to him
That made his horse a senator: each brim
Look big as mine: the gallant, jolly beast
Of all the herd – you'll say – was not the least.
Now crown the second bowl, rich as his worth
I'll drink it to; he, that like fire broke forth
Into the Senate's face, cross'd Rubicon,

And the State's pillars, with their laws thereon,
And made the dull grey beards and furr'd gowns fly
Into *Brundusium* to consult, and lie.
   This, to brave *Sylla*! why should it be said
We drink more to the living than the dead?
Flatt'rers and fools do use it: let us laugh
At our own honest mirth; for they that quaff
To honour others, do like those that sent
Their gold and plate to strangers to be spent.
   Drink deep; this cup be pregnant, and the wine
Spirit of wit, to make us all divine,
That big with sack and mirth we may retire
Possessors of more souls, and nobler fire;
And by the influx of this painted sky,
And labour'd forms, to higher matters fly;
So, if a nap shall take us, we shall all,
   After full cups, have dreams poetical.

Let's laugh now, and the press'd grape drink,
Till the drowsy day-star wink;
And in our merry, mad mirth run
Faster, and further than the sun;
And let none his cup forsake,
Till that star again doth wake;
So we men below shall move
Equally with the gods above.

Fida: Or the Country Beauty: to Lysimachus

Now I have seen her; and by *Cupid*
The young *Medusa* made me stupid!
A face, that hath no lovers slain,
Wants forces, and is near disdain.
For every *fop* will freely peep
At majesty that is asleep.
But she (fair tyrant!) hates to be
Gazed on with such impunity.
Whose prudent rigour bravely bears
And scorns the trick of whining tears:
Or sighs, those false alarms of grief,
Which kill not, but afford relief.
Nor is it thy hard fate to be
Alone in this calamity,
Since I who came but to be gone,
Am plagued for merely looking on.
    Mark from her forehead to her foot
What charming *sweets* are there to do't.
A *head* adorned with all those glories
That *wit* hath shadowed in quaint stories:
Or *pencil* with rich colours drew

In imitation of the true.
    Her *hair* laid out in curious *sets*
And *twists*, doth show like silken *nets*,
Where (since he played at *hit* or *miss*:)
The God of *Love* her prisoner is,
And fluttering with his skittish wings
Puts all her locks in curls and rings.
    Like twinkling stars her *eyes* invite
All gazers to so sweet a light,
But then two *arched clouds* of brown
Stand o'er, and guard them with a frown.
    Beneath these rays of her bright eyes
Beauty's rich *bed* of *blushes* lies.
Blushes, which lightning-like come on,
Yet stay not to be gazed upon;
But leave the *lilies* of her skin
As fair as ever, and run in:
Like swift *salutes* (which dull *paint* scorn,)
Twixt a *white* noon, and *crimson* morn.
    What *coral* can her *lips* resemble?
For hers are warm, swell, melt and tremble:
And if you dare contend for *red*,
This is *alive*, the other *dead*.
    Her equal *teeth* (above, below:)
All of a size, and *smoothness* grow.
Where under close restraint and awe
(Which is the maiden, tyrant law:)
Like a caged, sullen *linnet*, dwells
Her *tongue*, the *key* to potent spells.
    Her *skin*, like heaven when calm and bright,
Shows a rich *azure* under *white*,
With *touch* more soft than heart supposes,
And *breath* as sweet as new blown *roses*.

    Betwixt this *head-land* and the *main*,
Which is a rich and flowery *plain*:
Lies her fair *neck*, so fine and slender
That (gently) how you please, 'twill bend her.
    This leads you to her *heart*, which ta'en
Pants under *sheets* of whitest *lawn*,
And at the first seems much distressed,
But nobly treated, lies at rest.
    Here like two *balls* of new fallen snow,
Her *breasts*, Love's native *pillows* grow;
And out of each a *rose-bud* peeps
Which *infant* beauty sucking, sleeps.
    Say now my *Stoic*, that mak'st sour faces
At all the *Beauties* and the *Graces*,
That criest *unclean!* though known thy self
To every coarse, and dirty shelf:
Coulst thou but see a *piece* like this,
A piece so full of *sweets* and *bliss*:
In *shape* so rare, in *soul* so rich,
Wouldst thou not swear she is a witch?

Fida Forsaken

Fool that I was! to believe blood,
While swoll'n with greatness, then most good;
And the false thing, forgetful man,
To trust more than our true god, Pan.
Such swellings to a dropsy tend,
And meanest things such great ones bend.

Then live deceived! and, Fida, by
That life destroy fidelity.
For living wrongs will make some wise,
While Death chokes loudest injuries:
And screens the faulty, making blinds
To hide the most unworthy minds.

And yet do what thou can'st to hide,
A bad tree's fruit will be describ'd.
For that foul guilt which first took place
In his dark heart, now damns his face;
And makes those eyes, where life should dwell,
Look like the pits of Death and Hell.

Blood, whose rich purple shows and seals
Their faith in Moors, in him reveals
A blackness at the heart, and is
Turn'd ink to write his faithlessness.
Only his lips with blood look red,

As if asham'd of what they fed.
Then, since he wears in a dark skin
The shadows of his hell within,
Expose him no more to the light,
But thine own epitaph thus write
"Here burst, and dead and unregarded
Lies Fida's heart! O well rewarded!"

The Character, to Etesia

Go catch the *phoenix*, and then bring
A *quill* drawn for me from his wing.
Give me a maiden-beauty's *blood*,
A pure, rich *crimson*, without mud:
In whose sweet *blushes* that may live,
Which a dull verse can never give.
Now for an untouched, spotless *white*,
For blackest things on paper write;
Etesia at thine own expense
Give me the *robes* of innocence.
   Could we but see a *spring* to run
Pure *milk*, as sometimes springs have done,
And in the *snow-white* streams it sheds
Carnations wash their *bloody* heads.
While every *eddy* that came down
Did (as thou dost,) both *smile* and *frown*.
Such objects and so fresh would be
But dull resemblance of thee.
   Thou art the dark world's morning-star,
Seen only, and seen but from far;
Where like astronomers we gaze
upon the glories of thy face,
But no acquaintance more can have,
Though all our lives we watch and crave.

Thou art a world thy self alone,
Yea three great worlds refined to one.
Which shows all those, and in thine eyes
The shining *east*, and *Paradise*.
    Thy soul (a *spark* of the first *fire*,)
Is like the *sun*, the world's desire;
And with a nobler influence
Works upon all, that claim to sense;
But in *summers* hath no *fever*,
And in frosts is cheerful ever.
    As *flowers*, besides their curious *dress*
Rich *odours* have, and *sweetnesses*,
Which tacitly infuse desire
And even oblige us to admire:
Such and so full of innocence
Are all the *charms*, thou dost dispense;
And like fair *nature*, without *arts*
At once they seize, and please our hearts.
O thou art such, that I could be
A lover to idolatry!
I could, and should from heaven stray,
But that thy life shows mine the way,
And leave a while the *Deity*,
To serve his *image* here in thee.

To Etesia Looking From Her Casement at the Full Moon

See you that beauteous *Queen*, which no age tames?
Her train is *azure*, set with *golden* flames.
My brighter *fair*, fix on the *east* your eyes,
And view that bed of clouds, whence she doth rise.
Above all others in that one short hour
Which most concerned me, she had greatest power.
This made my *fortunes* humorous as wind,
But fixed *affections* to my constant mind.
She fed me with the *tears* of *stars*, and thence
I sucked in *sorrows* with their *influence*.
To some in *smiles*, and store of *light* she broke:
To me in sad *eclipses* still she spoke.
She bent me with the motion of her *sphere*,
And made me feel, what first I did but ear.
   But when I came to age, and had o'ergrown
Her rules, and saw my freedom was my own,
I did reply unto the laws of fate,
And made my reason, my great advocate:
I laboured to inherit my just right;
But then (O hear *Etesia*!) lest I might
Redeem my self, my unkind Starry mother
Took my poor heart, and gave it to another.

To Etesia (For Timander); the First Sight

What smiling star in that fair night
Which gave you birth gave me this sight,
And with a kind aspect tho' keen
Made me the subject, you the queen?
That sparkling planet is got now
Into your eyes, and shines below,
Where nearer force and more acute
It doth dispense, without dispute;
For I who yesterday did know
Love's fire no more than doth cool snow,
With one bright look am since undone,
Yet must adore and seek my sun.
   Before I walk'd free as the wind
And if but stay'd – like it – unkind;
I could like daring eagles gaze
And not be blinded by a face;
For what I saw till I saw thee,
Was only not deformity.
Such shapes appear – compar'd with thine –
In arras, or a tavern-sign,
And do but mind me to explore

A fairer piece, that is in store.
So some hang ivy to their wine,
To signify there is a vine.
   Those princely flow'rs – by no storms vex'd –
Which smile one day, and droop the next,
The gallant tulip and the rose,
Emblems which some use to disclose
Bodied ideas – their weak grace
Is mere imposture to thy face.
For Nature in all things, but thee,
Did practise only sophistry;
Or else she made them to express
How she could vary in her dress:
But thou wert form'd, that we might see
Perfection, not variety.
   Have you observ'd how the day-star
Sparkles and smiles and shines from far;
Then to the gazer doth convey
A silent but a piercing ray?
So wounds my love, but that her eyes
Are in effects the better skies.
A brisk bright agent from them streams
Arm'd with no arrows, but their beams,
And with such stillness smites our hearts,
No noise betrays him, nor his darts.
He, working on my easy soul,
Did soon persuade, and then control;
And now he flies – and I conspire –
Through all my blood with wings of fire,
And when I would – which will be never –
With cold despair allay the fever,
The spiteful thing Etesia names,
And that new-fuels all my flames.

To Etesia Parted From Him, and Looking Back

O, subtle Love! thy peace is war,
It wounds and kills without a scar,
It works unknown to any sense,
Like the decrees of Providence,
And with strange silence shoots me through,
The fire of Love doth fell like snow.
   Hath she no quiver, but my heart?
Must all her arrows hit that part?
Beauties like heav'n their gifts should deal
Not to destroy us, but to heal.
   Strange art of Love! that can make sound,
And yet exasperates the wound:
That look she lent to ease my heart,
Hath pierc'd it, and improv'd the smart.

Etesia Absent

Love, the world's life! what a sad death
Thy absence is! to lose our breath
At once and die, is but to live
Enlarg'd, without the scant reprieve
Of pulse and air; whose dull returns
And narrow circles the soul mourns.
   But to be dead alive, and still
To wish, but never have our will,
To be possess'd, and yet to miss,
To wed a true but absent bliss,
Are ling'ring tortures, and their smart
Dissects and racks and grinds the heart!
As soul and body in that state
Which unto us, seems separate,
Cannot be said to live, until
Reunion; which days fulfil
And slow-pac'd seasons; so in vain
Through hours and minutes – Time's long train –
I look for thee, and from thy sight,
As from my soul, for life and light.
For till thine eyes shine so on me,
Mine are fast-clos'd and will not see.

To Etesia Going Beyond Sea

Go, if you must! but stay – and know
And mind before you go, my vow.
` To every thing, but *heaven* and *you*,
With all my heart, I bid adieu!
Now to those happy *shades* I'll go
Where first I saw my beauteous foe.
I'll seek each silent *path*, where we
Did walk, and where you sat with me
I'll sat again, and never rest
Till I can find some *flower* you pressed.
That near my dying heart I'll keep,
And when it wants *dew*, I will weep:
Sadly I will repeat past joys,
And words, which you did sometimes voice:
I'll listen to the *woods*, and hear
The *Echo* answer for you there.
But famished with long absence I
Like *infants* left, at last shall cry,
And tears (as they do *milk*) will sup
Until you come, and take me up.

To His Books

Bright books! the *perspectives* to our weak sights:
The clear *projections* of discerning lights.
Burning and shining *thoughts*; man's posthume *day*:
The *track* of fled souls, and their *Milky-Way*.
The dead *alive* and *busy*, the still *voice*
Of enlarged spirits, kind heaven's white *decoys*.
Who lives with you, lives like those knowing *flowers*,
Which in commerce with *light*, spend all their hours:
Which shut to *clouds*, and *shadows* nicely shun;
But with glad haste unveil to *kiss* the sun.
Beneath you all is dark and a dead night;
Which whoso lives in, wants both health and sight.
   By sucking you, the wise (like *bees*) do grow
Healing and rich, though this they do most slow:
Because most choicely, for as great a store
Have we of *books*, as bees of *herbs*, or more.
And the great task to *try*, then know the good:
To discern *weeds,* and judge of wholesome *food,*
Is a rare, scant performance; for *man* dies
Oft ere 'tis done, while the *bee* feeds and flies.
But you were all choice *flowers*, all set and dressed
By old, sage *florists,* who well knew the best.
And I admit you all am turned a *weed*!
Not wanting knowledge, but for want of heed.
Then thank thy self *wild fool,* that wouldst not be
Content to know – what was too much for thee!

Distraction

O knit me, that am crumbled dust! the heap
    Is all dispersed, and cheap;
  Give for a handful, but a thought
      And it is bought;
      Hadst thou
Made me a star, a pearl, or a rain-bow,
    The beams I then had shot
    My light has lessened not,
      But now
I find my self the less, the more I grow;
      The world
Is full of voices; Man is called, and hurled
    By each, he answers all,
    Knows every note, and call,
      Hence, still
Fresh dotage tempts, or old usurps his will.
Yet, hadst thou clipped my wings, when confined in
    This quickened mass of sin,
  And saved that light, which freely thou
      Didst then bestow,
        I fear
I should have spurned, and said thou didst forbear;
    Or that thy store was less,
    But now since thou didst bless
      So much,
I grieve, my God! that thou hast made me such.
      I grieve?

O, yes! thou know'st I do' come, and relieve
    And tame, and keep down with thy light
    Dust that would rise, and dim my sight,
      Lest left alone too long
      Amidst the noise, and throng,
        Oppressed I
Striving to save the whole, by parcels die.

The Eagle

'Tis madness sure; and I am in the *fit*,
To dare an *eagle* with my *unfledg'd* wit.
For what did ever *Rome* or *Athens* sing
In all their *lines*, as lofty as his wing?
He that an eagle's *powers* would rehearse
Should with his plumes first feather all his verse.
   I know not, when into thee I would pry,
Which to admire, thy *wing* first, or thine *eye*;
Or whether Nature at thy birth design'd
More of her *fire* for thee, or of her *wind*.
When thou in the clear *heights* and upmost *air*
Dost face the sun and his dispersèd hair,
Ev'n from that distance thou the *sea* dost spy
And sporting in its deep, wide lap, the *fry*.
Not the least *minnow* there but thou canst see:
Whole seas are narrow spectacles to thee.
   Nor is this element of water here
Below of all thy miracles the sphere.
If poets ought may add unto thy store,
Thou hast in heav'n of wonders many more.
For when just *Jove* to earth his thunder bends,
And from that bright, eternal fortress sends
His louder volleys, straight this bird doth fly
To *Ætna*, where his magazine doth lie,
And in his active talons brings him more
Of ammunition, and recruits his store.
Nor is't a low or easy *lift*. He soars

'Bove *wind* and *fire*; gets to the *moon*, and pores
With scorn upon her duller face; for she
Gives him but shadows and obscurity.
Here much displeas'd, that anything like night
Should meet him in his proud and lofty flight,
That such dull *tinctures* should advance so far,
And rival in the glories of a star,
Resolv'd he is a nobler course to try,
And measures out his voyage with his eye.
Then with such fury he begins his flight,
As if his wings contended with his sight.
Leaving the moon, whose humble light doth trade
With *spots*, and deals most in the *dark* and *shade*,
To the day's royal *planet* he doth pass
With daring eyes, and makes the sun his glass.
Here doth he plume and dress himself, the beams
Rushing upon him like so many streams;
While with direct looks he doth entertain
The thronging flames, and shoots them back again.
And thus from star to star he doth repair,
And wantons in that pure and peaceful air.
Sometimes he frights the starry *swan*, and now
Orion's fearful *hare*, and then the crow.
Then with the *orb* itself he moves, to see
Which is more swift, th' *intelligence* or he.
Thus with his wings his body he hath brought
Where man can travel only in a thought.
   I will not seek, rare bird, what *spirit* 'tis
That mounts thee thus; I'll be content with this,
To think that Nature made thee to express
Our soul's bold *heights* in a material dress.

Discipline

Fair Prince of Light! Light's living Well
Who hast the keys of death and Hell!
If the mole man despise Thy day,
Put chains of darkness in his way.
Teach him how deep, how various are
The counsels of Thy love and care.
When acts of grace and a long peace,
Breed but rebellion, and displease,
Then give him his own way and will,
Where lawless he may run, until
His own choice hurts him, and the sting
Of his foul sins full sorrows bring.
If Heaven and angels, hopes and mirth,
Please not the mole so much as earth:
Give him his mine to dig, or dwell,
And one sad scheme of hideous Hell.

Midnight

I

      When to my eyes
(Whilst deep sleep others catches,)
      Thine host of spies
The stars shine in their watches,
      I do survey
      Each busy ray,
And how they work, and wind,
      And wish each beam
      My soul doth stream,
With the like ardour shined;
      What emanations,
      Quick vibrations
And bright stirs are there?
      What thin ejections,
      Cold affections,
  And slow motions here?

2

Thy heavens (some say,)
Are a fiery-liquid light,
     Which mingling aye
Streams, and flames thus to the sight.
      Come then, my god!
      Shine on this blood,
And water in one beam,
     And thou shalt see
   Kindled by thee
Both liquors burn, and stream.
     O what bright quickness,
     Active brightness,
And celestial flows
     Will follow after
     On that water,
Which thy spirit blows!

Peace

My soul, there is a country
   Far beyond the stars,
Where stands a winged sentry
   All skillful in the wars,
There above noise, and danger
   Sweet peace sits crowned with smiles,
And one born in a manger
   Commands the beauteous files,
He is thy gracious friend,
   And (O my soul awake!)
Did in pure love descend
   To die here for thy sake,
If thou canst get but thither,
   There grows the flower of peace,
The rose that cannot wither,
   Thy fortress, and thy ease;
Leave then thy foolish ranges;
   For none can thee secure,
But one, who never changes,
   Thy God, thy life, thy cure.

Mount of Olives (II)

When first I saw true beauty, and thy joys
Active as light, and calm without all noise
Shined of my soul, I felt though all my powers
Such a rich air of sweets, as evening showers
Fanned by a gentle gale convey and breathe
On some parched bank, crowned with a flowery
                                             wreath;
Odours, and myrrh, and balm in one rich flood
O'er-ran my heart, and spirited my blood,
My thoughts did swim in comforts, and mine eye
Confessed, *The world did only paint and lie.*
And where before I did no safe course steer
But wandered under tempests all the year,
Went bleak and bare in body as in mind,
And was blown through by every storm and wind,
I am so warmed now by this glance on me,
That, midst all storms I feel a ray of thee;
So have I known some beauteous *paisage* rise
In sudden flowers and arbours to my eyes,
And in the depth and dead of winter bring
To my cold thoughts a lively sense of spring.
Thus fed by thee, who dost all beings nourish,
My withered leaves again look green and flourish,
I shine and shelter underneath thy win
Where sick with love I strive thy name to sing,
Thy glorious name! which grant I may so do
That these may be thy *Praise*, and my *Joy* too.

Looking Back

Fair, shining *mountains* of my pilgrimage,
   And flowery *vales*, whose flowers were stars:
The *days* and *nights* of my first, happy age;
   An age without distaste and wars:
When I by thoughts ascend your *sunny heads*,
   And mind those sacred, *midnight* lights:
By which I walked, when curtained rooms and beds
   Confined, or sealed up others' sights:
      O then how bright
      And quick a light
   Doth brush my heart and scatter night;
      Chasing that shade
      Which my sins made,
   While I so *spring*, as if I could not *fade*!

How brave a prospect is a bright *back-side*!
   Where flowers and palms refresh the eye:
And days well spent like the glad *east* abide,
   Whose morning-glories cannot die!

Retirement

Fresh *fields* and woods! the Earth's fair *face*!
God's *footstool*! and man's *dwelling-place*!
I ask not why the first *believer*
Did love to be a country liver?
Who, to secure pious content,
Did pitch by *groves* and *wells* his tent;
Where he might view the boundless *sky*,
And all those glorious *lights* on high,
With flying *meteors*, mists, and *show'rs*,
Subjected *hills, trees, meads,* and *flow'rs*,
And ev'ry minute bless the King
And wise Creator of each thing.
   I ask not why he did remove
To happy *Mamre's* holy grove,
Leaving the *cities* of the plain
To *Lot* and his successless train?
All various lusts in *cities* still
Are found; they are the *thrones* of ill,
The dismal *sinks*, where blood is spill'd,
Cages with much uncleanness fill'd:
But *rural shades* are the sweet sense
Of piety and innocence;
They are the *meek's* calm region, where
Angels descend and rule the sphere;
Where Heaven lies *leiguer*, and the *Dove*
Duly as *dew* comes from above.
If *Eden* be on Earth at all,
'Tis that which we the *country* call.

The Revival

Unfold, unfold! take in his light,
Who makes thy cares more short than night.
The joys, which with his *Day-star* rise,
He deals to all, but drowsy eyes:
And what the men of this world miss,
Some *drops* and *dews* of future bliss.
   Hark! how his *winds* have changed their *note*,
And with warm *whispers* cal thee out.
The *frosts are past*, the *storms* are gone:
And backward *life* at last comes on.
The lofty *groves* in express joys
Reply unto the *turtle's* voice,
And here in *dust* and *dirt*, O here
The *lilies* o his love appear!

Regeneration

1

A ward, and still in bonds, one day
      I stole abroad,
It was high-spring, and all the way
    Primrosed, and hung with shade;
    Yet, was it frost within,
      And surly winds
Blasted my infant buds, and sin
    Like clouds eclipsed my mind.

2

Stormed thus, I straight perceived my spring
    Mere stage,a and show.,
My walk a monstrous, mountained thing
    Rough-cast with rocks, and snow;
    And as a pilgrim's eye
      Far from relief,
Measures the melancholy sky
    Then drops, and rains for grief,

3

So sighed I upwards still; at last
    'Twixt steps,a and falls
I reached the pinnacle, where placed
    I found a pair of scales,
    I took them up and laid
      In the one late pains,
The other smoke, and pleasures weighed
    But proved the heavier grains;

4

With that, some cried, *Away*; straight I
    Obeyed, and led
Full east, a fair, fresh field could spy
    Some called it, *Jacob's bed*;
    A Virgin-soil, which no
      Rude feet ere trod,
Where (since he stepped there,) only go
    Prophets, and friends of God.

5

Here, I reposed; but scarce well set,
    A grove escried
Of stately height, whose branches met
    And mixed on every side;
    I entered, and once in
      (Amazed to see't,)
Found all was changed, and a new spring

Did all my senses greet;

6

The unthrift Sun shot vital gold
  A thousand pieces,
And heaven its azure did unfold
  Chequered with snowy fleeces,
  The air was all in spice
   And every bush
A garland wore; thus fed my eyes
  But all the ear lay hush.

7

Only a little fountain lent
  Some use for ears,
And on the dumb shades language spent
  The music of her tears;
  I drew her near, and found
   The cistern full
Of divers stones, some bright, and round
  Others ill-shaped, and dull.

8

The first (pray mark,) as quick as light
  Danced through the flood,
But, the last more heavy than the night
  Nailed to the centre stood;

I wondered much, but tired
   At last with thought,
My restless eye that still desired
   As strange an object brought;

9

It was a bank of flowers, where I descried
   (Though 'twas mid-day,)
Some fast asleep, others broad-eyed
   And taking in the ray,
   Here musing long, I heard
   A rushing wind
Which still increased, but whence it stirred
   No where I could not find;

10

I turned me round, and to each shade
   Dispatched an eye,
To see, if any leaf had made
   Least motion, or reply,
   But while I listening sought
   My mind to ease
By knowing, where 'twas, or where not,
   It whispered; *Where I please*

   Lord, then said I, *On me one breath,*
   And let me die before my death!

The Request

O thou who didst deny to me
This world's ador'd felicity,
And ev'ry big imperious lust,
Which fools admire in sinful dust,
With those fine subtle twists, that tie
Their bundles of foul gallantry –
Keep still my weak eyes from the shine
Of those gay things which are not Thine!
And shut my ears against the noise
Of wicked, though applauded, joys!
For Thou in any land hast store
Of shades and coverts for Thy poor;
Where from the busy dust and heat,
As well as storms, they may retreat.
A rock or bush are downy beds,
When Thou art there, crowning their heads
With secret blessings, or a tire
Made of the Comforter's live fire.
And when Thy goodness in the dress
Of anger will not seem to bless,
Yet dost Thou give them that rich rain,
Which, as it drops, clears all again.
   O what kind visits daily pass
'Twixt Thy great self and such poor grass:
With what sweet looks doth Thy love shine
On those low violets of Thine,
While the tall tulip is accurst,

And crowns imperial die with thirst!
O give me still those secret meals,
Those rare repasts which Thy love deals!
Give me that joy, which none can grieve,
And which in all griefs doth relieve!
This is the portion Thy child begs;
Not that of rust, and rags, and dregs.

The Recovery

I

Fair vessel of our daily light, whose proud
And previous glories gild that blushing cloud;
Whose lively fires in swift projections glance
From hill to hill, and by refracted chance
Burnish some neighbour-rock, or tree, and then
Fly off in coy and wingèd flames again:
         If thou this day
         Hold on thy way,
Know, I have got a greater light than thine;
A light, whose shade and back-parts make thee shine.
Then get thee down! then get thee down!
I have a Sun now of my own.

II

Those nicer livers, who without thy rays
Stir not abroad, those may thy lustre praise;
And wanting light – light, which no wants doth
                            know –
To thee – weak shiner! – like blind Persians bow.
But where that Sun, which tramples on thy head,
From His own bright eternal eye doth shed
         One living ray,
         There thy dead day

Is needless, and man to a light made free,
Which shows that thou canst neither show nor see.
Then get thee down! then get thee down!
I have a Sun now of my own.

The Day-Spring

Early, while yet the *dark* was gay
And *gilt* with stars, more trim than day,
Heav'n's *Lily*, and the Earth's chaste *Rose*,
The green immortal *Branch* arose;
And in a solitary place
Bow'd to His Father His blest face.
   If this calm season pleased my *Prince*,
Whose *fulness* no need could evince,
Why should not I, poor silly sheep,
His *hours*, as well as *practice*, keep?
Not that His hand is tied to these,
From whom *Time* holds his transient *lease*
But *mornings* new creations are,
When men, all night sav'd by His care,
Are still reviv'd; and well He may
Expect them grateful with the day.
So for that first *draught* of His hand,
Which finish'd heav'n, and sea, and land,
The *sons* of God their thanks did bring,
And all the *morning stars* did sing.
Besides, as His part heretofore
The *firstlings* were of all that bore
So now each day from all He saves
Their soul's *first thoughts* and fruits He craves.
This makes Him daily shed and show'r
His graces at this early hour;
Which both His care and kindness show,

Cheering the good, quickening the slow.
As holy friends mourn at delay,
And think each minute an hour's stay,
So His Divine and loving *Dove*
With longing throes doth heave and move,
And soar about us while we sleep;
Sometimes quite through that *lock* doth *peep*,
And shine, but always without fail,
Before the slow sun can unveil,
In new *compassions* breaks, like light,
And *morning-looks,* which scatter night.
    And wilt Thou let Thy *creature* be,
When *Thou* hast watch'd, asleep to Thee?
Why to unwelcome loath'd surprises
Dost leave him, having left his vices?
Since these, if suffer'd, may again
Lead back the *living* to the *slain*.
O, change this *scourge;* or, if as yet
None less will my transgressions fit,
Dissolve, dissolve! Death cannot do
What I would not submit unto.

The World (II)

Can any tell me what it is? can you,
   That wind your thoughts into a *clue*
To guide out others, while your selves stay in,
         And hug the sin?
  I, who so long have in it lived,
     That if I might,
 in truth I would not be reprieved:
    Have neither sight,
   Nor sense that knows
    These *ebbs* and *flows*.
But since of all, all may be said,
  And *likeliness* doth but upbraid,
  And mock the *truth*, which still is lost
In fine *conceits*, like streams in a sharp frost:
  I will not strive, nor the *rule* break
  Which doth give losers leave to speak.
Then false and foul World, and unknown
      Even to thy own:
Here I renounce thee, and resign
Whatever thou canst say, is thine.
   Thou art not *truth*; for he that tries
Shall find thee all deceit and lies.
Thou art not *friendship*; for in thee
'Tis but the *bait* of policy.
Which, like a *viper* lodged in *flowers*,
Its venom through that sweetness pours.
And when not so, then always 'tis

A fading *paint*; the short-lived bliss
Of *air* and *humour*: out and in
Like *colours* in a *dolphin's* skin.
But must not live beyond *one day*,
Or *convenience*; then away,
Thou art not *riches*; for that *trash*
Which one age hoards, the next doth wash
And so severely sweep away;
That few remember, where it lay.
So rapid *streams* the wealthy *land*
About them, have at their command:
And shifting *channels* here restore,
There break down, what they banked before.
Thou art not *honour*; for those gay
Feathers will wear, and drop away;
And princes to some upstart *line*
Give new ones, that are full as fine.
Thou art not *pleasure*; for thy *rose*
Upon a *thorn* doth still repose;
Which if not cropped, will quickly shed;
But soon as cropped, grows dull and dead.
   Thou art the *sand*, which fills one *glass*,
And then doth to another pass;
And could I put thee to a stay,
Thou art but *dust*! then go thy way,
And leave me *clean* and bright, though *poor*:
Who stops thee, doth but *daub* his floor,
And *swallow*-like, when he hath done,
To *unknown dwellings* must be gone!
   Welcome pure thoughts and peaceful hours
Enriched with *sunshine* and with *showers*;
Welcome fair hopes and holy cares,
The not to be repented *shares*

Of time and business: the sure *road*
Unto my last and loved *abode*!
          O supreme *bliss*!
The circle, centre and abyss
Of blessings, never let me miss
Nor leave that *path*, which leads to thee:
Who art alone all things to me!
I hear, I see all the long day
The noise and pomp of the *broad way*;
I note their course and proud approaches:
Their silks, perfumes and glittering coaches.
But in the *narrow way* to thee
I observe only poverty,
And despised things: and all along
The ragged, mean and humble throng
Are still on foot, and as they go,
They sigh and say: *their Lord went so*!
    Give me my *staff* then, as it stood
When green and growing in the wood.
(Those *stones*, which for the *altar* served,
Might not be smoothed, nor finely carved:)
With this *poor stick* I'll pass the *ford*
As *Jacob* did; and thy dear *Word*,
As thou hast dressed it (not as *Wit*
And *depraved tastes* have poisoned it),
Shall in the passage be my meat,
And none else will thy servant eat.
Thus, thus and in no other sort
Will I set forth, though laughed as for't;
And leaving the wise *World* their way,
Go through, though judged to go astray

Illustrations

Including images of Henry Vaughan's homeland

Images of Herefordshire by J.M.W. Turner, this page and over.
River Wye, 1812 (above).

J.M.W. Turner, Tintern Abbey

A Note On Henry Vaughan

Henry Vaughan is the Metaphysical poet from the Welsh borders (he was born at Newton-upon-Usk, Breconshire, in 1621). He went up to Oxford, studied law in London, wrote some astonishing religious poetry, and died in 1695.

His poetry is marked by a 'deep, but dazzling darkness', as the poet writes in one of his most famous poems, 'The Night'. This dazzling night pervades Vaughan's poetry. It is a cosmic night, a night of regeneration. Many of the Vaughan's poems collected here pivot around an experience of the cosmic, religious night, from 'The World', with its famous, much-anthologized opening lines: 'I saw Eternity the other night/ Like a great *Ring* of pure and endless light'. It is a night of rebirth, the night as a dark womb, in which the world is reborn. Cosmic rebirth is one of the major themes in Vaughan's poetry, and especially in his collection or series of sacred poems, *Silex Scintillans*. 'Regeneration, the initial and dominant concern of *Silex Scintillans*, is a natural process: spiritual regeneration is approached and comprehended by drawing upon other and more immediately accessible modes of experience' writes Thomas O. Calhoun (p.128).

Vaughan is one of the most radiant of British poets. Like other Metaphysical poets (poets such as George Herbert, Richard Crashaw, Andrew Marvell and John Donne), the deep, dazzling darkness of the alchemical ferment in Vaughan's poetry is balanced by a radiance, a light shining out of the darkness. This is a divine light, as found in the *Mystical Theology* of that very influential writer, Dionysius the Areopagite. Dionysius' Neoplatonic visions of divinity and the celestial hierarchies of angels influenced Dante, among many others poets. In Dionysius, light and dark are used as elementary, primaeval manifestations of religious, cosmic forces, as in Gnosticism and Zorasterianism. It is not simply a case of God versus Satan, or good versus evil. That dualism is important in Neoplatonic and Christian philosophy, but it is not the whole picture. Instead, there is an emphasis on harmony, on the synthesis of opposites, which is a primary function of mythology and religion. Taoism has its *yin* and *yang* elements, where the dark contains the seed of the light, and vice versa. Each flows into the next. It is the same with Metaphysical poetry, and with Henry Vaughan. His poetry moves from dark to light, with the seeds of one being always present in the other. His nights, for all their darkness, also grow light.

Vaughan's poetry is about big themes, cosmic themes, religious themes, with titles such as 'The World', 'Regeneration', 'Peace', and 'The Retreat'. Vaughan is not shy of big themes, as some poets are. He dives right in. His openings are particular powerful, striking up a majestic tone immediately:

I saw Eternity the other night
Like a great *Ring* of pure and endless light... ('The World')

Happy those early days! when I
Shined in my Angel-infancy. ('The Retreat')

'My soul, there is a country
    Far beyond the stars... ('Peace')

They are all gone into the world of light!
    And I alone sit ling'ring here... ("They are all gone")

Through that pure *Virgin-shine*,
That sacred veil drawn o'er the glorious noon... ('The Night')

Stately lines these, which announce instantly the high-minded, serious, religious nature of the poems. Vaughan tackles, like the other Metaphysical poets, the grand themes of life: birth, death, love, God, faith, doubt, Nature and the self. His goal is rebirth, transformation, metamorphosis, call it what you will. Always there is movement in Vaughan's verse. As Helen O'Grady writes: 'At the level of sensory thought, Vaughan's emphasis is always on activity, the dynamic quality of impressions. His vital world is constantly moving, changing, a kaleidoscope of light and shadow and dynamic forms.'[1] It is a religious journey he takes us on, from confusion and insecurity through a night of shadows, a 'Dark Night of the Soul', to use St John of the Cross's term, to a final winning-through to harmony, even unity. Not all of Vaughan's lyrics are religious in Nature; indeed, we have included some of his 'secular' poems here, which deal in the more traditional, familiar manner with love. His religious poems, though, are his finest achievement, where he charts the 'progress of the soul'.

His poetry builds on a foundation of mysticism, the mysticism of Meister Eckhart, who spoke of going 'from nothingness to nothingness', and St John of the Cross, and visionaries such as Dionysius and Hildegard of Bingen. Whether Vaughan knew of these mystics or not is not our concern here: his poetry comes from that form of ecstatic, Christian mysticism.

Vaughan's Metaphysical philosophy is a combination of Christian and Neoplatonic thought. Vaughan's Neoplatonism include a variety of hermetic approaches. Most prominent, perhaps, is alchemy and pursuits associated with it – Rosicrucianism, for instance, and Western magic. Critics have written illuminatingly on the elements of magic and Neoplatonism in Shakespeare, the Elizabethans and the Metaphysical poets.[2] Henry and his brother Thomas were interested in various components of hermetic philosophy, including the great alchemist Paracelsus, the collection of writings called 'Hermes Trismegistus',

---

1 Quoted in Rudrun: *Henry Vaughan*, 62.
2 See, for example: Ted Hughes: *Shakespeare and the Goddess of Complete Being*, Faber 1992; Frances Yates: *The Rosicrucian Enlightenment*, Routledge 1972 and *Giordano Bruno and the Hermetic Tradition*, Vintage Books, New York 1969; D.P. Walker: *Spiritual and Demonic Magic from Ficino to Campanella*, Warburg Institute 1958; Wayne Shumaker: *The Occult Sciences in the Renaissance*, University of California Press, Berkeley, Calif., 1972; Walter Pagel: *Paracelsus: An Introduction to Philosophical Medicine in the Era of the Renaissance*, Karger, New York 1958; Peter French: *John Dee*, Routledge 1972.

Cornelius Agrippa's *De Occulta Philosophia*, the alchemical treatise *Theatricum Chemicum*, and the *Oracles* of Zoroaster.[3]

There is not space here to deal in depth with the hermetic/ Neoplatonic/ alchemical elements in Vaughan's poetry. Usually the Metaphysical poets are viewed in relation solely to Christian thinking. But the more one finds out about them, the more their philosophy tends towards the alternatives to Christianity – alchemy, Neoplatonism, magic, numerology, Rosicrucianism, Qabbalism, and so on. Indeed, these philosophies all operate within the Judaeo-Christian tradition, and poets do not see any conflict, necessarily, between the 'One and All' of Neoplatonism and the God of Judaeo-Christianity. Renaissance philosophy brought together Christianity and pantheism, Christianity and Neoplatonism. Poets see unity, and multiplicity in unity. For them, there is not necessarily a conflict between Nature worship and God worship. For Vaughan, pantheistic, Nature mysticism is not at odds with monotheic Christianity. All things, rather, are united – in Vaughan's case by the visionary experience of the poet.

In Vaughan's work, we are always aware of the sky, the vast, wheeling sky, as with Shakespeare and Rilke. Vaughan's sky is, of course, filled with celestial music, the 'music of the universe' as Boethius called it.[4] There is music in Nature, a harmony. There is a song in the heart of the world, poets believe, and Vaughan sings it. 'Song is existence' as Rilke wrote in his *Sonnets to Orpheus*. Many poets have sung the song of Nature, much as the ancestor-gods of the Australian aborigines 'sung' the world into existence. At this primal level, at the level of Creation mythologies, poetry and music fuse, forming a continuum embodied in one figure, the shaman.

The world's mysteries can be 'sung' by the poet. 'The poet, like the alchemist, can make Nature "speak"' writes Thomas Calhoun in his study of Vaughan (106). The poet discovers them, or simply uncovers them so that people can experience them. They were always there. Life is always rich, even blissful. One simply has to

---
[3] See Rudrun: *Henry Vaughan*, 4; Calhoun, 53f; Martin; Durr.
[4] Boethius: *De institutione musica*, 1.3, in Gottfried Friedlin: *Source Readings in Music History*, ed Oliver Strunk, Norton, New York, 1950, 86.

be aware of it. Poets such as Vaughan, Rilke, Goethe, Rimbaud and Spenser try to make these mysteries or 'streams' of life, as the poet Peter Redgrove calls them,[5] clear to all. These sound like very high-flown claims, yet Henry Vaughan is always a poet who deals, like Crashaw or Hardy, in 'serious' themes.

It's romantic, perhaps, to think that Vaughan's Nature mysticism was inspired partly by his surroundings, the hills and vales of Wales, which are very beautiful. Alan Rudrun writes:

> This quality in Vaughan's poetry is related, one feels sure, to the fact of his living in the Usk Valley, with its shifting sunshine, cloud and shower and the incessant sound of running water...[6]

When we look at Vaughan's poetry, we see an immense love of Nature and natural forms. Not just skies, but flowers, mountains, rivers, and so on. Vaughan's Nature poetry, though, is overlaid or, rather, powered by a radiant language. So rivers are not mere channels of water, but shining ribbons winding through the world. Clouds are not simply clouds, they are golden clouds. Vaughan's Nature poetry becomes, all the time, symbolic. His poems feature protagonists who are on pilgrimages, who travel through a world lit by 'pure Virgin-shine'. The 'Virgin-shine' is a good term, laden with mystery, to define the light that suffuses Vaughan's poetry. His poems are descriptions of what the poet sees during his voyages through the 'Virgin-shine' world.

Look at 'Looking Back': it is typical of Vaughan's work, featuring a pilgrimage through a religious landscape, a landscape at once natural and magical. Vaughan throws a religious radiance around landscapes, so they glow. So 'To His Books', he opens with 'Bright books!', and in 'Midnight' he describes heaven as a 'fiery-liquid light'. Everywhere there is radiance in Vaughan, but this radiance has to gained and won, after the struggle through the Dark Night of the Soul. The ecstasy, when it comes, is intense, as ecstasies tend to be. 'The Morning-Watch' is a poem of 'coming through', as D.H. Lawrence put it. It is a poem of extreme joy, like Rimbaud's 'Morning of Ecstasy' from his *Illuminations*.

---
[5] See Peter Redgrove: *The Black Goddess and the Sixth Sense*, Bloomsbury 1987.
[6] Rudrun: *Henry Vaughan*, 63.

Metaphysical poetry is full of extreme statements, often of religious rapture, and often accompanied by exclamation marks. True, Shelley and Keats use more exclamation marks than Vaughan or Donne, but in 'The Morning-Watch', Vaughan celebrates his rebirth in grand style:

> O joys! infinite sweetness! with what flowers,
> And shoots of glory, my soul breaks, and buds!
>   All the long hours
>   Of night, and rest
>   Through the still shrouds
>   Of sleep, and clouds,
> This dew fell on my breast...

Vaughan's poetry is optimistic, at times idealistic, if being alive to life is being idealistic. His poetry is, ultimately, a poetry of celebration, whereas many other poets end up moaning negatively about life, without offering any remedies. Vaughan of course is a believer, and his faith in God buoys him up in his darkest moments. He does not dredge the depths of despair, as some mystics have done. He sees God in Nature and celebrates this vision.

Bibliography

Don Cameron Allen: "Henry Vaughan's 'Salome on Ice'", *Philological Quarterly*, 23, 1944, 84-5
—. "Henry Vaughan: "Cock Crowing", *Image and Meaning: Metaphoric Traditions in Renaissance Poetry*, John Hopkins University Press, Baltimore 1960
Edmund Blunden: *On the Poems of Henry Vaughan: Characteristics and Intimations*, Richard Cobden-Sanderson 1927
Robert E. Bourdette: "Recent Studies in Henry Vaughan", *English Literary Renaissance*, IV no.2, 1974, 299-310
Thomas O. Calhoun: *Henry Vaughan: The Achievement of* Silex Scintillans, University of Delaware Press/ Associated University Press, New Jersey 1981
A.U. Chapman: "Henry Vaughan and magnetic philosophy", *Southern Review* (Adelaide), IV, iii, 1971, 215-26
R.A. Durr: *On the Mystical Poetry of Henry Vaughan*, Harvard University Press, Cambridge, Mass., 1962
Kenneth Friedenreich: *Henry Vaughan*, Twayne Publishers, Boston 1978
Ross Garner: *Henry Vaughan: Experience and Tradition*, University of Chicago Press, Chicago 1959
Elizabeth Holmes: *Henry Vaughan and the Hermetic Philosophy*, Blackwell 1932
Merritt Y. Hughes: "The theme of pre-existence and infancy in 'The Retreat'", *Philogical Quarterly*, XX, 1941, 484-500
F.E. Hutchinson: *Henry Vaughan: A Life and Interpretation*, Clarendon Press, 1971
A.CC. Judson: "The Source of Henry Vaughan's Ideas Concerning God in Nature", *Studies in Philology*, XXIV, 1927, 592-606
Frank Kermode: "The Private Imagery of Henry Vaughan", *Review of English Studies*, N.S., 1, 1950
E.L. Martin: "Henry Vaughan and 'Hermes Tristmegistus'", *Review of English Studies*, 18, July 1942, 302-4
—. "Henry and Thomas Vaughan", *Modern Language Review*, 39, 1944, 180-3

W.R. Parker: "Henry Vaughan and his Publishers", *The Library*, 4th series, 20, 1940, 40`1-6

Jonathan F.S. Post: "Vaughan's 'The Night' and his 'late and dusky' Age", *Studies in English Literature*, 19, 1970, 127-141

Mary Eileen Rickey: "Vaughan, *The Temple*, and Poetic Form", *Studies in Philology*, 59, 1962, 162-170

Alan Rudrun: *Henry Vaughan,* University of Wales Press, 1981

—. "The Influence of Alchemy in the Poems of Henry Vaughan", *Philological Quarterly*, 49, 1970, 469-80

—. "Henry Vaughan's 'The Book': a hermetic poem', *Journal of the Australian Universities Language and Literature Association*, 1961, 161-6

—. "Henry Vaughan and the theme of transfiguration", *Southern Review*, I, 1963, 54-68

—. "Vaughan's 'The Night': some hermetic notes', *Modern Language Review*, LXIV, 1969, 11-19

J.D. Simmonds: *Masques of God: Form and Theme in the Poetry of Henry Vaughan*, University of Pittsburgh Press, Pittsburgh, 1972

A.J. Smith: "Henry Vaughan's Ceremony of Innocence", *Essays and Studies*, N.S., 26, 1973, 35-52

E.M. Williamson: *Henry Vaughan*, Welsh Home Service 1953

CRESCENT MOON PUBLISHING

ARTS, PAINTING, SCULPTURE

The Art of Andy Goldsworthy: Complete Works
Andy Goldsworthy: Touching Nature
Andy Goldsworthy in Close-Up
Andy Goldsworthy: Pocket Guide
Andy Goldsworthy In America
Land Art: A Complete Guide
The Art of Richard Long: Complete Works
Richard Long: Pocket Guide
Land Art In the UK
Land Art in Close-Up
Land Art In the U.S.A.
Land Art: Pocket Guide
Installation Art in Close-Up
Minimal Art and Artists In the 1960s and After
Colourfield Painting
Land Art DVD, TV documentary
Andy Goldsworthy DVD, TV documentary
The Erotic Object: Sexuality in Sculpture From Prehistory to the Present Day
Sex in Art: Pornography and Pleasure in Painting and Sculpture
Postwar Art
Sacred Gardens: The Garden in Myth, Religion and Art
Glorification: Religious Abstraction in Renaissance and 20th Century Art
Early Netherlandish Painting
Leonardo da Vinci
Piero della Francesca
Giovanni Bellini
Fra Angelico: Art and Religion in the Renaissance
Mark Rothko: The Art of Transcendence
Frank Stella: American Abstract Artist
Jasper Johns
Brice Marden
Alison Wilding: The Embrace of Sculpture
Vincent van Gogh: Visionary Landscapes
Eric Gill: Nuptials of God
Constantin Brancusi: Sculpting the Essence of Things
Max Beckmann
Caravaggio
Gustave Moreau
Egon Schiele: Sex and Death In Purple Stockings
Delizioso Fotografico Fervore: Works In Process 1
Sacro Cuore: Works In Process 2
The Light Eternal: J.M.W. Turner
The Madonna Glorified: Karen Arthurs

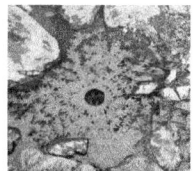

LITERATURE

J.R.R. Tolkien: The Books, The Films, The Whole Cultural Phenomenon
J.R.R. Tolkien: Pocket Guide
Tolkien's Heroic Quest
The *Earthsea* Books of Ursula Le Guin
Beauties, Beasts and Enchantment: Classic French Fairy Tales
German Popular Tales by the Brothers Grimm
Philip Ullman and *His Dark Materials*
Sexing Hardy: Thomas Hardy and Feminism
Thomas Hardy's *Tess of the d'Urbervilles*
Thomas Hardy's *Jude the Obscure*
Thomas Hardy: The Tragic Novels
Love and Tragedy: Thomas Hardy
The Poetry of Landscape in Hardy
Wessex Revisited: Thomas Hardy and John Cowper Powys
Wolfgang Iser: Essays and Interviews
Petrarch, Dante and the Troubadours
Maurice Sendak and the Art of Children's Book Illustration
Andrea Dworkin
Cixous, Irigaray, Kristeva: The *Jouissance* of French Feminism
Julia Kristeva: Art, Love, Melancholy, Philosophy, Semiotics and Psychoanalysis
Hélène Cixous I Love You: The *Jouissance* of Writing
Luce Irigaray: Lips, Kissing, and the Politics of Sexual Difference
Peter Redgrove: Here Comes the Flood
Peter Redgrove: Sex-Magic-Poetry-Cornwall
Lawrence Durrell: Between Love and Death, East and West
Love, Culture & Poetry: Lawrence Durrell
Cavafy: Anatomy of a Soul
German Romantic Poetry: Goethe, Novalis, Heine, Hölderlin
Feminism and Shakespeare
Shakespeare: Love, Poetry & Magic
The Passion of D.H. Lawrence
D.H. Lawrence: Symbolic Landscapes
D.H. Lawrence: Infinite Sensual Violence
Rimbaud: Arthur Rimbaud and the Magic of Poetry
The Ecstasies of John Cowper Powys
Sensualism and Mythology: The Wessex Novels of John Cowper Powys
Amorous Life: John Cowper Powys and the Manifestation of Affectivity (H.W. Fawkner)
Postmodern Powys: New Essays on John Cowper Powys (Joe Boulter)
Rethinking Powys: Critical Essays on John Cowper Powys
Paul Bowles & Bernardo Bertolucci
Rainer Maria Rilke
Joseph Conrad: *Heart of Darkness*
In the Dim Void: Samuel Beckett
Samuel Beckett Goes into the Silence
André Gide: Fiction and Fervour
Jackie Collins and the Blockbuster Novel
Blinded By Her Light: The Love-Poetry of Robert Graves
The Passion of Colours: Travels In Mediterranean Lands
Poetic Forms

POETRY

Ursula Le Guin: Walking In Cornwall
Peter Redgrove: Here Comes The Flood
Peter Redgrove: Sex-Magic-Poetry-Cornwall
Dante: Selections From the *Vita Nuova*
Petrarch, Dante and the Troubadours
William Shakespeare: *The Sonnets*
William Shakespeare: Complete Poems
Blinded By Her Light: The Love-Poetry of Robert Graves
Emily Dickinson: Selected Poems
Emily Brontë: Poems
Thomas Hardy: Selected Poems
Percy Bysshe Shelley: Poems
John Keats: Selected Poems
D.H. Lawrence: Selected Poems
Edmund Spenser: Poems
Edmund Spenser: *Amoretti*
John Donne: Poems
Henry Vaughan: Poems
Sir Thomas Wyatt: Poems
Robert Herrick: Selected Poems
Rilke: Space, Essence and Angels in the Poetry of Rainer Maria Rilke
Rainer Maria Rilke: Selected Poems
Friedrich Hölderlin: Selected Poems
Arseny Tarkovsky: Selected Poems
Novalis: *Hymns To the Night*
Paul Verlaine: Selected Poems
Arthur Rimbaud: Selected Poems
Arthur Rimbaud: *A Season in Hell*
Arthur Rimbaud and the Magic of Poetry
D.J. Enright: By-Blows
Jeremy Reed: Brigitte's Blue Heart
Jeremy Reed: Claudia Schiffer's Red Shoes
Gorgeous Little Orpheus
Radiance: New Poems
Crescent Moon Book of Nature Poetry
Crescent Moon Book of Love Poetry
Crescent Moon Book of Mystical Poetry
Crescent Moon Book of Elizabethan Love Poetry
Crescent Moon Book of Metaphysical Poetry
Crescent Moon Book of Romantic Poetry
Pagan America: New American Poetry

MEDIA, CINEMA, FEMINISM and CULTURAL STUDIES

J.R.R. Tolkien: The Books, The Films, The Whole Cultural Phenomenon
J.R.R. Tolkien: Pocket Guide
The *Lord of the Rings* Movies: Pocket Guide
The Cinema of Hayao Miyazaki
Hayao Miyazaki: *Princess Mononoke*: Pocket Movie Guide
Hayao Miyazaki: *Spirited Away*: Pocket Movie Guide
Tim Burton
Ken Russell
Ken Russell: *Tommy*: Pocket Movie Guide
The Ghost Dance: The Origins of Religion
The Peyote Cult

Cixous, Irigaray, Kristeva: The *Jouissance* of French Feminism
Julia Kristeva: Art, Love, Melancholy, Philosophy, Semiotics and Psychoanalysis
Luce Irigaray: Lips, Kissing, and the Politics of Sexual Difference
Hélène Cixous I Love You: The *Jouissance* of Writing
Andrea Dworkin
'Cosmo Woman': The World of Women's Magazines
Women in Pop Music
Discovering the Goddess (Geoffrey Ashe)
The Poetry of Cinema

The Sacred Cinema of Andrei Tarkovsky
Andrei Tarkovsky: Pocket Guide
Andrei Tarkovsky: *Mirror*: Pocket Movie Guide
Andrei Tarkovsky: *The Sacrifice*: Pocket Movie Guide
Walerian Borowczyk: Cinema of Erotic Dreams
Jean-Luc Godard: The Passion of Cinema
Jean-Luc Godard: *Hail Mary*: Pocket Movie Guide
Jean-Luc Godard: *Contempt*: Pocket Movie Guide
Jean-Luc Godard: *Pierrot le Fou*: Pocket Movie Guide
John Hughes and Eighties Cinema
Ferris Bueller's Day Off: Pocket Movie Guide
Jean-Luc Godard: Pocket Guide

The Cinema of Richard Linklater
Liv Tyler: Star In Ascendance
Blade Runner and the Films of Philip K. Dick
Paul Bowles and Bernardo Bertolucci
Media Hell: Radio, TV and the Press
An Open Letter to the BBC
Detonation Britain: Nuclear War in the UK
Feminism and Shakespeare
Wild Zones: Pornography, Art and Feminism
Sex in Art: Pornography and Pleasure in Painting and Sculpture
Sexing Hardy: Thomas Hardy and Feminism

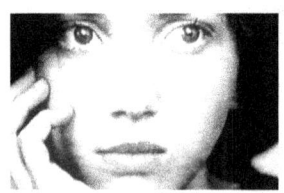

In my view *The Light Eternal* is among the very best of all the material I read on Turner. (Douglas Graham, director of the Turner Museum, Denver, Colorado)

The Light Eternal is a model monograph, an exemplary job. The subject matter of the book is beautifully organised and dead on beam. (Lawrence Durrell)

It is amazing for me to see my work treated with such passion and respect. (Andrea Dworkin)

CRESCENT MOON PUBLISHING
P.O. Box 1312, Maidstone, Kent, ME14 5XU, Great Britain. www.crmoon.com